AN ARTIS
SURVIVAL GUIDE

Lessons Learned the Hard Way about Making Art

So You Won't Have to

_____

Malcolm Dewey

An Artist's Survival Guide

Copyright © 2017 by (Malcolm Dewey Fine Art)

ISBN 9781521464717

Published Linspire 124 CC t/a (www.malcolmdeweyfineart.com)

Dedication

To Kerrin and the boys.

And to artists everywhere who show up and do their work every day.

Contents

Discover More

If you are the curious type and are interested in other projects I have been involved in, you may want to click on the links below. You will discover books, courses and other bits and bobs that I get up to when not painting (I know, I should paint more ☺)

Free Offer

Learn to Paint With Impact

How to Loosen Up Your Painting

From Acrylics to Oil Painting in 5 Easy Steps

How to Solve Painting Problems

An Artist's Guide to Plein Air Painting

The Art of Content Marketing

My Artist's Blog

Introduction

Catchy title right? Coming up with a presumptuous title like *An Artist's Survival Guide* is typical of my delusions of grandeur. A noble quality for every artist in my opinion. So is a penchant for tongue-in-cheek remarks. Oh well, carry on.

Truth is I would love to get up to glamorous survival feats like Bear Grylls does and live to write about them. Sadly I am too lazy to jump out of helicopters (chicken too) and I hate the taste of beetle pate.

I could see myself as a fictional hero like Jack Reacher, but that would mean learning self-defence techniques from experts so that I could write about them. This is sure to entail sweating and accidental punches to my throat. Way too risky.

Instead I decided to give up a career in law and follow my passion for painting. So not risky at all then. Crikey!

But here I am still kicking and doing okay too. Maybe I did learn a few things about creating art, painting for a living and having fun along the way.

I have collected a series of ideas, thoughts, tips and observations over the years and included them in this short book. Some heart-felt and others irreverent, but all part of my journey. I do hope you find a few useful nuggets amidst the other bits.

Sincerely

Malcolm

Chapter One: How Do You Know You Are an Artist?

What a question? This is the sort of thing some artists want to know from other annoyed artists. It usually ends up in an argument with both artists convinced that the other is a complete twit. And has not a shred of artistic ability. The end.

But wait. Maybe this is not the correct question at all. What is lying deep down in every insecure artist's mind is this: Will other people believe that I am an artist? Or will they dismiss me as a delusional imposter?

An artist is anyone who creates something from an idea of some sort. It can be a book, a film, a painting, a spiral staircase, a tiffany lamp and very many other things.

I am sure most think of the fine arts like painting and sculpture when the word artist is used. But artist is a wide notion so please do not be offended if I talk about painters. It is simply what I know best. The process and struggles are similar for all artists.

My first recollection of artistry was drawing a cartoon from an image on a shoebox. How pedestrian! But it was amusing to my six year old mind and more importantly I received praise from adults for my work. Hang on! I could enjoy drawing cartoons and get kudos for drawing them from grown-ups. Seemed like a good deal at the time. Nothing much has changed over forty years later come to think of it.

And that is where the trap lies. Artists want affirmation through praise, sales, galleries, publishers, likes, shares and so forth. Heck I want it all. But what happens when you do not get all of that attention? Are you still an artist?

Or what if you are doing art as a side hustle while you are an accountant by day. Is art just a hobby for you? That is like the kiss of death to your aspirations as an artist.

Moving on from there do you have to be a professional to be considered a serious artist?

Now that we have established some of the neuroses of artists in Chapter One perhaps there will be a few answers in the forthcoming chapters. I cannot wait to find out.

Onward!

Chapter Two: Make Way for the Artist

When I started blogging with some earnest in June 2012 I had grand ideas for the blog. I created a forum page to encourage artists to share their experiences and I wanted to shake things up a bit. A quote from article number one:

"This site has more focus on art products, techniques, daily artist's process and hopefully some feedback from artists. I do hope that this fresh approach gets things stirred up a little!"

With hindsight I did learn that a forum was a non-starter. The work to supervise it even when the visitors numbered two (and one was me) was considerable. But trying to rustle up sufficient interest among local artists was the most soul destroying process. Nobody wanted to start a topic and nobody wanted to be the only one responding to a topic that I started. Reasonably I suppose, but still hard to swallow when I had such high hopes.

Lessons learned:

1. Focus on main issue. Your Art

2. Do not expect other part time and hobby painters to be as madly passionate about painting as you are. They have their own priorities.

3. Do not throw money after bells and whistles like forum hosting, for example, when you need money for essentials like more paint, food and so on.

4. Repeat Item 1 above

PS: Focus does not mean to lose the fire, passion and expression of your heart. On the contrary it is on these things that your focus should be aimed.

"If I create from the heart, nearly everything works: if from the head, almost nothing."

Marc Chagall

Chapter Three: Know the Value of Painting

Digital is great - no doubt about that. My website, my extensive photo references and business run on digital. However it still is like comparing a plastic dashboard to one of walnut veneer or vinyl to leather.

We cannot do without the synthetic stuff, but we also need the real thing. That is what makes a painting so special. It is handmade, tangible, textured and old school. Prints and photos do not have the esoteric quality of a painting.

There is no comparison to the considered, technical and spiritual demands required for a painting to succeed. Sometimes a painting feels like it is born out of state of consciousness that cannot be replicated. No matter how I try to paint another similar painting it is impossible.

That is what attracts me back to the easel. The struggle, the joy the rebirth of something unique. Once complete the painting must be passed on unselfishly to a new owner and I start another. It is a journey and cannot be ignored.

What is the value of a painting when there are basic needs not being met in this world? You can decide for yourself. Perhaps in this world of instant gratification the ancient arts and creative spirit is all that humans can fall back on to make sense of it all.

1. Be grateful for creating and enjoying art. Perhaps one of human being's highest achievements especially since art and love are so closely connected.

Chapter Four: Find Your Muse amid the Clutter

What is the battle fought by every artist? I would hazard a stab at the old enemy *procrastination*. I would also include *cluttered thoughts* to the list.

The muse visits when the mind is uncluttered and clutter stems from a cluttered life. Or in this case a cluttered studio? There is no doubt that clearing out physical clutter frees the mind as well. Try it for yourself and do not put it off. It is a liberating experience.

My studio got to the point where I would bump into things on the floor, books piled up haphazardly and old, abandoned paintings stacked up against the wall. All of this irritated me and that interfered with my focus on the easel.

Once the penny dropped it was clear that something drastic had to be done. Clear out everything not useful! No, not perhaps useful *one day*. Everything that I would not use this week, if I needed to, had to get binned!

Typical examples: paintbrushes that have been worn down; dirty, unused jars, cans, paint tubes untouched for months, painting panels waiting "to be finished", magazines (where do they all come from!) papers, receipts and so on. Do not even think of dissecting art magazines for useful pics for a scrapbook. It is a delusion! Chuck it out.

What about half finished paintings abandoned with the hope of a miraculous revelation leading to completion. Burn them! There is a reason for them not being completed - you were on the wrong path and your muse has shown you a better way. IT HURTS BUT YOU WILL PAINT BETTER PAINTINGS!

The lesson learned from this process? (For it is a process not just a once off event)

An immediate lightening of my mood and liberation of the creative muse. (Two great paintings were completed shortly thereafter)

Chapter Five: Success at Art is Like Eating Oatmeal

It has been cold lately. One of our colder winters people say considering we are on the east coast of South Africa where winter never means frost and such. One of my favourite breakfasts on these chilly mornings is oatmeal porridge - With honey and cinnamon and a bit of milk the way my wife makes it - even my kids like it!

As good as those oats smell though you can only eat it one way. That is one small spoon at a time from the top. Dive right in with big spoonfuls like a famished farmhand and you are going to get burned. Every time.

Thing is though after a while the oatmeal cools and you can carry on and chances of burning diminish. So obviously I thought:" Hang on **this is like trying to build an art career.**" Stay with me - I can explain.

My former day job meant days at a desk working papers, phone calls, research, consulting and administration. I compare this to a winter's morning, just not the pretty kind, but the dry biting cold and bleached look that makes you think that spring is taking its jolly time getting here.

The prospect of spending mornings preparing to paint and then attacking the canvas with bright colours is like the fragrant bowl of oatmeal - comforting and restorative.

Here's the rub though. **Many artists dive right into the business of art and get burned.** With their hopes up and the joy of painting fuelling their spirits they put their work out there and experience the unexpected pain of rejection.

It can come in many ways and hurts for longer than an oatmeal burn.

The artist is then at a crossroads. Pack up the easel and brushes and put them in a corner. Kid yourself that you will get back to painting this weekend but conveniently find other tasks to do? After a while painting is no longer a part of your future. There will always be rationalisations to back this up whether from well-meaning people or anecdotes about other artists getting burned.

But you are not one to pack it in so fast. At the back of your mind **you know that your day job is a soul-sucking existence.** You know that when you get to the final curtain call there is no rewind button like on your satellite TV. This is your one shot at life and you are going to be true to your calling. Your God given nature needs to create. It is the one thing that feels right and true.

The beauty of this **decision to follow your creative path** is that once made all the naysaying suddenly looks weak and toothless. How did you let other's words hurt you so much? The fact is that truth is always more powerful than lies. Lies get exposed even when you are lying to yourself.

You get on with it then, but this time you take a more considered approach. You read the books, practice, learn from others who have walked the path of their calling and create with increased assuredness.

Your confidence grows and your art responds. You rebuild and then try again. This time you have some success. It only takes a moment to fuel your calling. You will know it even if others are blind to it. This is for you alone. Savour it and move forward one moment at a time.

Will there be more painful moments? Maybe - rejection certainly, but will rejection hurt you? Unlikely because you have seen the enemy and defeated him once before. You know what to do.

Lessons learned:

1. Take your time and learn more;

2. Take advice from others with a pinch of salt;

3. Eat oatmeal

Chapter Six: When in Doubt Read a Book

Not just any book though. Something that can help you along your journey. One such book that I can modestly endorse for artists is Robert Henri's book *The Art Spirit*.

Is there an antidote for the cynical world we live in? How many times do you second guess yourself, your art and your choice to paint?

As an artist I can relate to the need for calm and self-affirmation. It will be okay. Keep on creating. In this reflective moment I find the writings of Robert Henri in *The Art Spirit* a comforting reminder that artists have asked these questions for a long time. It is a reminder that art is timeless. The Art Spirit is indeed a record of the human spirit triumphant.

The Art Spirit records Henri's anecdotes, philosophy and practical art knowledge. Robert Henri (1865-1929) was a famous French artist and teacher who settled in America. In his time he came into contact with many famous masters and passed on his knowledge by teaching to many others who in turn went on to become masters.

"There are moments in our lives, there are moments in a day, when we seem to see beyond the usual. Such are the moments of our greatest happiness. Such are the moments of our greatest wisdom. If one could but recall his vision by some sort of sign. It was in this hope that the arts were invented. Sign-posts on the way to what may be. Sign-posts toward greater knowledge."
-Robert Henri

This is not a book of glib soundbites. It is not a quick read filled with platitudes that can be glossed over. **This is a book that must be read slowly and absorbed**. Give yourself time to think about what Henri is saying. Read a page of two every day if you like to gain some calm and reflection over what art really means to you.

Despite the depth of ideas and sincerity in the writer I was moved by the **similarity of concerns that artists** experienced over a hundred years ago. Many issues are no different today. His advice is just as relevant today and a reminder that we share much in common with those who went before and thrived in struggle. Consider this quote:

"Just remember that the object of painting pictures is not simply to get them in exhibitions. It is all very fine to have your pictures hung, but you are painting for yourself, not for the jury. I had many years of rejections."

Would I recommend this book to an artist? Yes - read it and go back to it when you are in need of solace and calm. This too shall pass and there is much joy to be found when the human spirit triumphs over the banality of life. Art is merely the evidence of this journey.

Chapter Seven: Is Busyness Stealing Your Creativity?

Busyness - the state of being or appearing to be actively engaged in an activity.

- **Have you found yourself wondering where the day has gone with little to show for it?**
- Are you spending too much time being distracted?
- Is your creative time becoming less due to time in front of a screen?

I have been busy lately, but there is that uneasy feeling of not being able to show much for it. To be honest I need to take some of my own medicine and get back to work on time every day. The hard truth is that it is very easy to spend too much time keeping up with the distractions that crop up.

Heaven help if these distractions become habits. It is time to focus!
Identify the culprits. These time-bandits include:

- Checking e-mail too often
- Updating any form of social network
- Reading too many blogs (mine excepted of course:)
- Surfing the net for fun before the work is done
- Newspapers or news online
- Unnecessary shopping online or off

This list can easily wipe out two hours of your day.

This reminds me of the time I sat through two hours of the *John Carter* DVD. I will never get that time back and it annoys me no end.

Research in front of the computer often turns into surfing for stuff we do not need. Oh, hang on – my smartphone beeped – just a second – new e-mails – I will check them quickly ….
What! Lunch already?

The beauty of art is that it is analogue. We need to remember this. Creating can be kept simple if we keep our focus. Get to the easel and draw or paint. Creativity is a state of focus. A Zen state that is within our grasp. The sad thing is that distractions become habits, which rob us of this state of focus. The good news is that positive habits can be adopted. It is a decision.

"Nature does not hurry, yet everything is accomplished."
- Lao Tzu

This wonderful quote is a wake up moment for me. I am a landscape artist first and foremost so I must appreciate the timeless rhythms of nature. The grace and beauty of nature doing what it has done since the creation. I can choose to respect nature by turning away from distractions.

I realise that this need to focus goes hand in hand with simplification. Simplify is a mantra that needs repeating when painting, but also needs to be part of the artist's lifestyle. We must decide that we want a simpler life.

It requires effort at first then becomes a habit. Give it a month. We each know our vices – our time-bandits. Saying "Do the work" is not enough. We need a conscious decision to make a simpler approach to life possible.

22

Small steps – for example: e-mail program is not opened until midday or perhaps switched off at 9am until 4pm. You decide, but be bold.

To Do:

1. Consider what distracts you;
2. Simplify by eliminating all things that get in the way of your work;
3. Do ONE thing today that will help you simplify your life

Chapter Eight: The Interview that Started the Dream

Do you believe in dreams? Not the bedtime variety, but the stuff you want to happen with your life kind of dreams. I am not sure if I do or not. I tend to look at future wants as goals. You know if you want something badly enough you set goals to achieve them?

Not necessarily fancy goals with checklists and time tables. But a goal nonetheless. I find this helps me to achieve things. But looking back at how I got into painting fulltime makes me think that I am a dreamer that sometimes has dreams come true.

I was still at law school. It was in the evening and I was probably procrastinating about some assignment while listening to the radio (old tech cause this was in the late 80's). I remember the next event clearly though. An interview with an artist came on and grabbed my attention like a fist-full of T-shirt.

The artist was talking about his art and then the interviewer asked the artist why he decided to stop practicing law and go into professional art. Everything stood still at that moment and I thought this cannot be. An attorney changing career to professional artist was an idea that blew my young mind.

A bit of background – I had studied art at school, taken the lessons and let's just say that I doodled a few trees worth of paper in my early days. When career choices came up I went to the art-related career evenings, but they all emphasised industrial arts, which did not fire me up.

I was also not into fashion design. Fine art as a career? Oh no! That was not on the career counsellor's list! So I chose law obviously.

Fast forward a few years and here is someone who did the whole law career and then gave it up. Brilliant – he had to be crazy. But there he was talking about the joy he was now having following his dream.

Who was he? To this day I cannot be sure. I think my mind was just processing the idea and I did not recall much else. If I had to guess I would suggest that it was Dale Elliott (that great South African artist who was an attorney once). This seems likely and I have certainly been inspired by Dale Elliott's story. Maybe one day Mr Elliot can confirm whether it was indeed him being interviewed.

Looking back is always instructive as patterns begin to emerge. There were so many small yet important markers along the way. Is it a coincidence that I purchased one of Dale's prints as a young attorney and then many years later visited his studio and there was the same print framed prominently in front of me?

Not to mention how so many other events fell into place leading to where I am today effectively living the same idea I heard over twenty years ago. Was it "attraction" or karma or just the natural development of things?

I am not a fatalist, but I do believe that what we decide upon is not always a rational conscious state of mind. It is our true selves that makes the decision and we find ourselves on a certain path. Do you follow that path? The decision determines whether you remain a dreamer of someone whose dreams come true.

But be warned. You may get what you asked for.

Chapter Nine: Parting with Your Paintings is Hard but Necessary

A professional does the work and sells the painting. That is the artist's calling and he must answer loud and clear. It sounds like a nice enough job – get up, think about a project or maybe get out for some reference work. Then start in the studio and push on through the day. A steady stream of painting sales keeps the wolf from the door.

If all does go according to plan and the muse is in full force I will be really pleased with a couple of paintings a month that have taken me to a new level. Admittedly it is progress by degrees, but progress nevertheless. Is it tempting to keep a painting back? Do I want to hang onto a painting that has won my heart perhaps with the promise that I will put it out there sometime in the future? The answer is yes, but I still put it up for sale.

I know an artist who likes to select a painting that he is particularly happy with. He keeps that one aside and calls it his retirement plan. I think this is a mistake. A great painting must not be hidden away, but must be put out there to build the artist's career. It is very likely that over time the artist will move on with his painting style. He may no longer have the feelings he once did for the painting. Now it looks long in the tooth. He cannot sell it now.

Once I made the decision to go pro a different thought pattern emerged. I chatted to artist, Daniel Novela, about this. He admitted that it was hard to part with a few special paintings, but he still had them on display for sale.

Once a painting is complete there is an energy that has been released and must be passed on. The process then begins anew. Failing to do this will hold an artist back. Holding onto a painting for resale in years to come like some kind of pension feels wrong and self-defeating.

What artist does not get pleasure in sharing the collector's excitement? It is all good. Paint it with an open heart and let go.

Chapter Ten: Tales from a Gallery

Do you want to open your own gallery? Think about it. You can sell your own paintings to adoring fans. No more worries about distribution or reaching out to other galleries that don't care about your work. Sounds good, right?

I spent a year marketing my art in a bricks-and-mortar art gallery. This was an experiment and since the lease was for just one year I thought, what the heck? Let's do it.

My experience through that period was invaluable. I had the pleasure of meeting different artists and collectors. I experienced the highs and lows of the art trade.

I also have respect for hard working gallery owners. It is not an easy business. A good gallery owner will appreciate the artists who are true to their profession and will also treat customers with the respect they deserve.

After a year it was time for me to devote my energy to creating both at the easel and through writing about art. I learned that being a shop keeper was not my thing. Since overheads have to be kept low I was not ready to employ others either. You see the problems?

Now I have the pleasure of meeting many good people through my online gallery and writing for good people like you.

Here are some of the highs and lows and a few lessons learnt during this time as a gallerist:

- Making the first sale of the week to a young couple on a Thursday afternoon just before closing time brought a lump to my throat. My spirit was restored, but I learnt that I cannot fix my emotions on the sale. An artist must create. Then focus on the business of sales. The two are different things

- To the ladies who came into the gallery to stare at and debate the merits of the wall colour before deciding that it would indeed look good in their lounge – I hope you discover that paintings on the walls will do far more for your décor!

- To the gent who stood in the doorway staring into the gallery, with a smug look, and commented that "you guys must be struggling these days" then turned and walked away – no my friend, we leave the struggle to those who cannot see.
- Getting used to the phrase "I want to buy it, but I must ask my husband/wife" They never buy it – trust me.

- I had a laugh at one young lady who came in with her camera and asked if she could photograph a painting I did because she wanted to paint something like it for her house. Bless her, she didn't bat an eyelid and I did not have the heart to say no. After all I accepted the request as a compliment.

- My favourite collector was a lady who knew what she wanted. She would regularly walk in and head directly for the large painting, point at it and declare "I will take this one!" Then whip out the credit card and the deal was done in five minutes. Brilliant!

- The most pleasure comes from those sales that mean so much to the collector. The man who was moved to tears by a painting because the clouds reminded him of the day his mother passed away. Still gets to me.

- Or the couple who saved up to buy their special painting and seeing their joy and excitement – priceless.

- Or the tourists who went to the trouble of getting their paintings shipped to the UK because the paintings would remind them of their wonderful time in South Africa. I love you guys!

- Another favourite collector would make regular visits and seldom left without a painting or at least an encouraging word to me. Always reminding me to keep at it and assuring me of greater success. He did not have to say those things, but art moved his soul. Thank you Dries.

- Phoning an artist to tell them that their painting has sold and sharing their joy – always special.

- To those folk who would say thank you just because they could look at some original art. It is always a pleasure. Thank you!

Chapter Eleven: Carrot or Stick. What Works for You?

If a list of mankind's greatest achievement is drawn up then the humble book must surely be near the top. Just under the internal combustion engine and anaesthetics probably.

On a slow Saturday afternoon with the children yelling at each other and my wife's internal barometer dropping fast to stormy I decided to bundle the lot into the car and head off to Bargain Books. This made everyone very happy. On arrival we all split up and went on our individual treasure hunt looking for that special book.

As I wandered through the aisles I passed that curious section called Esoterica. There are all sorts of books about spiritual wellness. Tai chi, meditation, mystical beliefs and other practices that would have had you tied to a stake not so long ago.

What stood out after a bit of browsing were the box sets. These attractively packaged sets offer peace, harmony and enlightenment if you listen to the CD and read the little book that comes with it.

Seven steps to nirvana. Find your inner joy in 14 days. All have one thing in common. They emphasise the good things that will happen to you. The carrot that makes us reach for the credit card.

Unfortunately these happy events are too vague to keep us going. What is peace, inner joy and harmony? Different things to different people I expect. It is no wonder that these books and CDs end up in the car-boot sales practically untouched.

What is it that gets us to do the work that brings us benefits later? Could it be the nasty consequences if we don't crack on with it? Perhaps we would follow the meditation course if the book was titled "Meditate or Die Prematurely". There are probably studies on this.

The art section has similar promises of quick results. If you want to learn how to draw quickly and easily then you are spoilt for choice. Some books come with pencils and sketch books too, which will save you time on your journey to drawing excellence.

I suggested to my wife that she try one of these drawing books, but she replied that she could already draw like Picasso then started laughing. She can be funny that way.

The world needs more artists, but there is just not enough stick to make it worthwhile for most. You see most folks go to work because if they don't they get fired and then there is no money. This makes the children unhappy. Most of us can endure miserable jobs on this system.

But **what if our work promised joy, peace and fulfilment**. Imagine if we could do the work that made us happy. What if it was all carrot and we did not have to worry about the stick anymore?

Oh there would still be things to buy and bills to pay, but instead of making these things central to our system we could focus on what we are passionate about. The obligations would still be met. We would have less debt certainly, because we would not feel the need to fill up our empty lives with junk on credit. This might just work.

I will let you know once I have finished listening to my CD.

Chapter Twelve: Seeing No Progress in Your Painting? Try This

Take a look at children's art. Children's art is usually based on what they know. Although colours and proportions may not be accurate children paint what is important to them. Family, pets, their home and friends or special moments. The result is often touching yet spontaneous and expressive.

Adult beginners will often choose subjects they like but know nothing about. For example are you painting Cape winelands scenes when you live on the coast? Despite you only seeing the winelands perhaps once every few years when on holiday? Perhaps you rely on painting winelands scenes from photos out of magazines.

No wonder that the painting lacks feeling and leads to disappointment.

In case you think I am being judgmental let me confess that I have painted adlib scenes like this in my early days too. It is natural that we want to paint scenes that we find beautiful. It is okay to practice and painting is better than not painting at all right? But if you want to make real progress you will have to move on to real subjects that you know well. This advice is often told to writers, but applies to painters too.

I see many paintings from beginners that bear no emotional bond with their own experience. The artist is frustrated and uncertain about whether her art is good enough. The artist is not making a breakthrough because the subject is too detached.

The personal link is missing and without that emotional connection there is no real art.

Beautiful mountain views of the Rockies will have no resonance with someone living in the Karoo for instance. So why paint them? Paint the Karoo if you live there. Let us take a moment to consider the impressionists. Those intrepid artists who ventured outdoors with canvas and tubes of paint determined to seek the truth in everyday scenes.

What about the abstract artist or expressionist? Yes painting in the studio may make sense, but this could apply to the representational artist too. Consider **Van Gogh** whose scenes became increasingly expressionist yet were painted in most cases en plein air.

He still painted what he saw yet this did not hinder his emotional expression. **Gauguin** too based his work on scenes and figures he observed first hand. Even **Picasso's *Les Demoiselle d'Avignon*** was based on actual women he observed. This did not hinder Picasso painting them in his cubist manner.

If you find yourself painting in a second hand fashion I would like to challenge you to venture outdoors and paint a local scene up close and personal. Another option is to take out your photo album and find scenes that resonate with you. That you experienced first-hand.

Sketch a tight scene, plan the composition then paint it. You will find more pleasure from this and begin to really see the colours and values because they are familiar. You will also discover that more painting opportunities will reveal themselves once you mind and eye start seeking them out.

Tip:

1. Start with sketches in pencil or charcoal. Leave the painting out of it until you have the composition ironed out.

2. Use pencil and watercolour wash to start feeling the colours. It is about building momentum and planning too.

3. When ready you can unleash your paints on the canvas.

Chapter Thirteen: First Steps in Art Sales? Try Local Markets and Fairs Part 1

Art fairs are excellent places to start selling your art. Here's why:

1) **Cost of entry is low**. Yes, let us get this out of the way. The entry fee is low compared to any form of rented space and the outlay on preparing your stand is also low. Nobody expects Persian carpets and other decor. However this does not mean that you can get away with a nasty market stand either. More on this in part two.

2) **People like to meet the artist**. This is just human nature and it is great for you the artist. Believe it or not there is a certain curiosity about artists. This can range from "Who is this master?" to "How do artists make a living?" Whatever the angle meeting and chatting to an artist is usually an interesting experience for visitors to your stall.

3) **The benefit for the artist** is that he can get immediate feedback from visitors, make connections and gain confidence in speaking about art. It is important to be able to articulate your ideas about art without launching into a thesis or getting tongue tied.

4) **You may meet a gatekeeper**. This is anybody who can get you further access to marketing events or exposure that will benefit your art marketing. This could be a gallery event, newspaper article, corporate commission, art lesson candidates and so on. It is probably unlikely that a big time collector will buy out your stand, but all things are connected. You are starting something that could lead to great things.

5) **You start to develop a brand**. I assume that you are calling yourself an artist and that you are not apologising for your art. As such it is essential that you develop yourself as a brand. Your name is now associated with art and you can build on this brick by brick. I would strongly suggest that you trade under your own name and not some cute name even if it may sound catchy at first. This will save you much hassle later when your business takes off.

6) **You will learn about collectors**. Yes how people react to art is a lesson in life. Some will not get your art. Others will swoon over it. Most will be interested and appreciative. You will learn how to cope and deal with each of these and more. This will help to build your fortitude for the challenges that lie ahead. No one said it would be easy, but there are also blissful moments that will have you smiling for days.

I recall my first market where one moment I had someone laughing at a price I had set for a painting and the next person purchasing two paintings. That is the way it goes. No point in getting upset and no point in compromising either.

7) **You will learn to negotiate**. Compromise is not negotiation. You will need to negotiate sometimes to make a sale. Prepare for this and accept it as essential. Collectors love to buy art and they love to negotiate. It does not mean they will not respect you, but negotiation is part of the fun. Accept it and prepare your strategy.

Oh yes, did I mention you will learn about being a salesperson? This is good. You will need this quality throughout your art career whether or not you have a gallery representing you. You are your business so best get educated in the art of the sale too.

8) **You may sell a painting or two**. Yes you may but it could be at a later date. If you are present and show an interest in people visiting your stand then you have an above average chance of making a sale. You may also be able to follow up with a potential buyer later on.

9) **You develop stamina**. After a day at a market you will be exhausted. This will give you strength and humility. You will prepare better next time. You will also appreciate getting back to your studio and **feel motivated** to up your game.

10) **You start to gather an all-important contact list**. More of this in part 2.

Action Step:

Find a market or fair that you can attend this year. Take a leap of faith and sign up for it.

Prepare yourself, but do not make this a be-all-and-end-all. Not all market events are equal and it pays to pick and choose the best, however it will give you momentum and that is when things start to happen.

Chapter Fourteen: Try Local Markets and Fairs Part 2

You have decided to go for it so how can you maximise on the opportunity. If you do not approach the event with intention you will very likely have a long and boring day.

So here are **ten suggestions** based on personal experience.

1) **Attend in person:** Sounds obvious, but it is very tempting for studio loving artists to rope in as many helpers as possible to "mind the store". The argument runs along the lines that you are an artist not a salesperson, talking is not your forte and so forth. (I had to get over this issue myself).

If you are selling you need sales skills. Folks want to meet the artist and most importantly only you know your art inside and out. Speaking from experience I can attest to becoming a chatterbox about art even though I am a bit of an introvert. It's my passion and it's yours too so trust your knowledge.

2) **Presentation:** A few basic improvements to how you present your work will pay for themselves. A few touches add class. For example a good looking table cloth adds class to a cheap pine table. Also consider the following.

3) **Signage:** Try to get a sign made professionally. This could be a canvas sign or banner with your name, website address and possibly a logo. It will also describe what you do, for example, Malcolm Dewey *Fine Art*. You may come up with other creative methods, but make sure people can tell at a glance who you are and what you do.

4) **Framing:** do you need to frame your art? If so then go for it. Too expensive? Then frame a few anchor pieces and offer others unframed with a framing option. Price accordingly.

Framing helps tremendously so if you go this route do not skimp by using cheap and skinny frames. It's a tricky matter, but there it is. Emphasise the benefits of buying with a frame and you will sell the framed painting. Emphasise the benefits of buying unframed and you could make those a success too.

5) **Display Stands:** There is no need to buy expensive easels. A bit of basic woodworking can produce basic display easels. Trellis can be used to hang paintings on hooks too. Convert an old wooden ladder into a tiered easel. **Be creative and you will save costs and gain positive responses**.

6) **Quality over quantity**. This a balancing act. Too much and a sense of clutter follows. Too little and your stall may look the poorer for it. However quality always comes first. Art fairs do not means you should try selling your lesser quality work.

7) **Comfort:** If indoors is it necessary or even possible to install better lighting? Maybe a fan will help with comfort in summer? Here are more tips about canopies and tents for your stall.

8) **Marketing:** **This is critical** and it is all about give and take. Give your business card with your website and phone details. Better still send them your info digitally once you get their contact info.

Forget about expensive flyers or brochures - they do not work. **Get visitor's contact details then follow up with e-mail to those who expressed interest in you**. Run a giveaway for those who give out their contact info and email.

Free gifts or some other benefit such as discounts on art lessons, discount on your next book, paintings you name it. Just do not pass up the opportunity to get future networking links. Make it easy by having a short form visitors can complete. An enlarged GR code prominently displayed? Do your best to prepare **your system** to get emails and build a list.

I want to emphasise the word SYSTEM. If you are selling then you need a system that works for your business.

9) **Price:** Price your art according to its value. Do not compete on price. Your art is unique - show its value and benefits to the collector. Price normally. Give discounts - **negotiate**, but do not compromise.

I price my paintings on a sum per centimetre measured diagonally across the painting. This ensures that large paintings are not too high compared to smaller ones. If you simply work on square-centimetre pricing then larger paintings show massive price jumps. Measuring the diagonal line from top to bottom corner solves this problem.

10) **Payment:** Since your art may be beyond the usual cash amounts carried around you will need to consider electronic payment options. If this is out of the question your other option may be to arrange for payment by electronic transfer and deliver the painting later.

Tricky this as sales can fall away very quickly. If technology does not scare you then look into wireless computing whether on laptop, tablet or smart phone.

Several online service providers offer credit card processing online using smartphones. Some require you to have a merchant account with a bank others do not.

Times are changing fast and card scanners are now small portable devices. Of course there is the traditional merchant account credit card machines from one of the big banks, but that could mean long term costs and much hassle.

Tip:
Be as self-reliant as possible!

PS: This is not as daunting as it looks. Try it for yourself. Sure there are short cuts like simply leaning a few paintings against the fence and hoping for the best. But if you are in this for the long haul then do the best you can with what you have to create a great impression.

Chapter Fifteen: The Grateful Artist

I confess that I like Mondays. This does go against convention apparently. Mention this in conversation and polite people smile indulgently. If they are less polite I usually get a derisive snort and reasons why Mondays are not favoured.

Mondays give me the opportunity to start putting into action what I thought about on the weekend. This is key. Taking time off on the weekend to think and plan gets me ready for action on Monday.

Weekends are for relaxing I hear you say. True, but relaxing and quiet contemplation go hand in hand. They get my creative juices flowing. I am grateful for this.

I am grateful that I do not face Mondays with dread for what lies ahead. I think of those entering cubicle hell, perhaps fearful confrontations with a mad boss, customers, bank managers, teachers, creditors or even real danger such going down a mine. Or general drudgery.

I am grateful that many of these jobs are performed for our benefit and the greater good. It would be a happier world however if the folks carrying out these jobs loved their work. Unfortunately many do not. This makes Mondays a dreadful day for many. It is very sad.

I have read and been told how important gratitude is in our lives. I have heard that true creativity can only reach a higher plane if accompanied by a grateful heart. I agree with this. I have first-hand experience of it.

Good things happen when accompanied by good thoughts and positive action. Some call it serendipity. Fortuitous timing.

There are a few things I know for sure about gratitude. The success of my day depends upon it. If I choose to let events bring me down and I lose my sense of gratitude. I am no longer able to create effectively or at all. This drags me down further until my sole aim is simply to get to the next day. Can you relate? How many times have you said to yourself: "I cannot wait for this day to end" "Tomorrow cannot come too soon." The day is a write off!

Of course there are events of significant distress that will ruin a day. But these are few and far between. We are often sabotaging our days with idle events. Little things to moan about. These are our **energy killers**.

Artists have a way of dealing with this. They can get to work. Whether preparing a canvas, cleaning the studio (note to self: may become procrastination) or getting down to the main event - making art. This is where we must express our gratitude.

Our ability to work and thus to live our passion is something to be grateful for. It is the flow of the universe through our creative actions that makes time disappear and the moment all supreme. It could not happen without gratitude.

Gratitude for the air we breathe, our health, our senses, our ability to see the world and appreciate the incredible energy that created this all. Let us be grateful for something and focus on that.

Ignore the purveyors of bad news, whether they come in print, TV or in person. You will allow your inner self to find freedom from the clamour of an ungrateful world.

This will give your natural creative self a moment to come forward. The energy will be felt again as channels for its graceful flow are reopened. Have your pencils, brushes or whatever you need close at hand. You will soon be creating again.

PS: Look up the fabulous song by Nina Simone called *I Got Life.* A statement about gratitude for what you have.

Chapter Sixteen: The Grateful Artist Part 2

The positive response to my recent article titled *The Grateful Artist* has been a lesson in the human condition. It has also shown me perhaps for the first time in my life that gratitude is possibly the most powerful force we humans can access. What about love you may ask. What is love if you are not grateful for it to begin with?

My journey through art has been long, but it is perhaps only the past several years that I have become fully aware of this gift. There is a huge rift between the blind stumble that I went through for so long. Undervaluing the gifts that we have or not seeing them at all.

It is one of our human frailties that we take too much for granted. We are creatures of habit they say. Familiar steps every day make us feel secure, but like pinballs we bounce off the hard knocks until we are practically sleep walking.

I did hear talk of **gratitude opening people's eyes to their own potential.** In the past that message did not sink in. Now I get the picture. I have also seen that there is a real need for so many people to wake up and realise their own potential. I firmly believe that it begins with gratitude.

Fortunately gratitude does not require a big outlay. No fancy clothes, car or house is required. No degrees or endorsements and no entrance fee. Just you and I acknowledging that there is a purpose to our lives. There is something to be grateful for.

Life as an artist became possible when I took a risk. The risk still occasionally scares me now. It meant confronting a fear and going ahead anyway. For me it was not simply about putting my paintings before the public. It meant a gamble with my family responsibilities and long term future.

You do not have to take a financial risk if you are an artist. Your art can be a side business or simply a creative outlet. Forget what others think of you. It is what you do that matters. And sharing your art the way you think is best is where you need to begin.

Would I take it personally if someone scoffed or if the paintings were ignored completely? Was I merely a pretender? It is much safer to stay out of sight, but that is damaging on so many levels.

Not taking the risk would have been ungratefulness. We are all given something positive to offer the world and keeping it to ourselves is just not on. Fortunately **fear is weak when confronted** and gratefulness keeps the fear away. My worries were baseless. I did the work and let go of the angst.

Another shock to me has been the spontaneous goodwill that so many people have offered me. I have not asked for things yet they have been given. I have tried to give something of value and it has come back to me multiplied. Is there a catch?

Real life still goes on. I still have to pay bills and get up and get to work. The difference is in the choices that open up when you are doing the work that was meant for you. You can say no, but it seems that I get to say yes more often to what I ask for.

Perhaps with more awareness I see more opportunity. Sometimes I still want to blame coincidence rather than anything esoteric like fulfilment of my soul's purpose.

Awareness - with this comes the right to choose and be grateful.

When I finish typing this I will continue with my new painting. It is a moment to accept and gently acknowledge with gratitude. What tomorrow brings is a mystery, but I have today and it is good.

Tip: Start a gratitude journal. Or add a gratitude prayer at the dinner table tonight. Get the family involved. A mini-Thanksgiving every day.

Chapter Seventeen: Art is Energy so Make Some

The world of physics was in raptures recently. An invisible bit of energy exposed itself to a computer in a very expensive tunnel. No one could see this happening, but they can infer that something that was not there before had come and gone. Someone with a beard and a laboratory coat could explain this better than me. However this little slip of energy has been called the Higgs-Boson. A sub-atomic particle so small that you wouldn't notice it even if it passed right through you.

It is easy to discount such things, but energy is perhaps the most important part of the universe. We are so connected to energy in its infinite forms that it is everything we are and will be forever. That is a long time indeed.

This keyboard I am bashing on, the screen from which you will read this and everything else for that matter is energy. So what has this to do with art? All this energy has one purpose it seems and that is to create.

Energy creates things, conditions of being and even emotions. Disease for example is simply energy gone bonkers. Antibiotics is another form of energy designed to wipe out the crazy diseased energy or at least change it into something non-threatening.

All of this energy works in fine balance and when out of kilter things go wrong.

Eastern medicine calls energy chi and has ways to help you unblock energy pathways. Blocked energy leads to all sorts of unpleasant ailments. Energy must more freely and cannot be lost either. We try to store energy for example in batteries, but they run down anyway. Especially when you need them the most.

Creativity. Let us consider how we create with energy all day long without even knowing it. Your expression, the words you use, the words you read, the tone of your voice and even your thoughts however well disguised give off energy. This affects you and those within your energy field.

My wife gets angry with me at times presumably for something that I do that negatively affects her chi. Then she affects my chi most negatively indeed. Once our chi is unblocked we share a glass of wine together and all is well again.

Energy is transferred across the world merely by what is communicated every second. Consider how you feel when you rashly turn on the news and see some form of madness perpetrated in another time zone. Instant what? Anger, fear, compassion, dread? Then consider how you feel when a loved one smiles at you or you receive a compliment. Positive energy flows through you instantly.

That is the part that knocks my socks off. Instant energy. You do not have to think about feeling good. It just happens. What happens then? We transfer this positive energy to others instantly. Energy flows and you cannot stop it until you let negative vibes back in.

So let us accept the idea that the universe consists of energy. **Creative energy is the tool used by the universe to make everything and the energy is infinite**. We are energy highways. We accept energy instantly and transmit it just as instantly without effort.

The universe creates non-stop whether by way of a volcano or a honey bee in the orchard. Everything in linked in some way. A butterfly flaps its wings in one part of the planet and someone falls off a chair in another part of the planet.

As artists our work and inspiration is positive energy. Sublime and beautiful. Fulfilling a purpose beyond perception. Do not let others attack this idea with negativity. So too must we refrain from responding with negativity to other's creative efforts. The transfer of energy through our actions and onto others who appreciate our work is nothing less than a God given purpose. This energy heals and restores. It connects us to our souls.

Let us be aware and accepting. Let us make that energy count.

Chapter Eighteen: Climbing Out of a Creative Rut

One of my artist friends asked me what I do when I find myself stuck in a creative rut. I was in one of those periods recently. Not the first time and it will not be the last either. Every artist gets into a creative rut at times. The good news is that these ruts are necessary. They are a call to up your game.

The artist's rut has many causes. Perhaps the most common are:

- Doing the same technique over and over and expecting a different result (this may also signal madness)
- Painting the a subject without a purpose;
- Failing to study your art;
- Not painting regularly;
- Painting too much;
- Other physical or emotional problems causing weariness or distraction;
- Not changing your environment or references;
- Professional bondage to one style or subject is creative death;
- An art problem that cannot be resolved;

You may recognise the feeling of being in a rut when you approach painting without that old fizz. That state of happiness that starts quietly and builds up to being blissfully in the moment. Time stands still and you are doing the work. When these qualities are missing it can be depressing. Are you losing your touch? Have you reached the bottom of your talent quota?

No you are fine. **You are ready for the next step up.**

The typical issues for me are related to subject and technique. Sounds mundane enough. Just change them and you are okay. Not so fast. Getting to this point of recognising the problem, resolving to change something and acting upon it is not simple. It takes energy and discipline. You have to give yourself the proverbial kick in the pants. Make your bargains with the painting gods and get your energy flowing.

Here are a few techniques that help:
1. Get outside and take a walk.

Walk with purpose and vigour. See your surroundings like an artist. Look for shapes, values. Breathe in deeply. Breathe out the frustrations.
If you cannot take a walk then any form of exercise that raises your breathing and heart rate will have good effect. Energy flows from action.

2. If you have an idea then go with it. Draw it out in simple form. Then put it aside. Let it develop in your mind for a while.

3. While the energy is starting to kick in I like to **stoke the fire** a bit more by going through preparations. Hands on tasks like preparing painting panels. Cutting canvas. Priming. I line up the panels and will prime ten or more. Get out a white canvas and tone it.

I am not going to start a painting at this point even if I am tempted to. I tell myself the best is still to come. The breakthrough moment will be tomorrow, but I will be prepared.

Come the morning and I am painting with purpose. Music on. Big brush. Big shapes. Once that canvas has the blocking in completed I start another and block it in too.

This is all about action and bold movement. I do not want to get stuck on middle and end stages of a painting. I know I will be ready for those later in the day or the next day.

4. Look at your subject and technique. Change something. Just do it and go with it. If you have been painting landscapes then paint a portrait. Use big brushes and paint in broad planes to sculpt the face. Loose and free. Those same broad strokes will be used in your next landscape.

Change colours. Paint an entire painting using tones of burnt sienna for example. If I like what I see I may add more colour over the monotone and the painting will go in another direction.

I am out of the rut and it has made me stronger. That is what ruts are good for. The most important point is always to get moving. Hustle yourself along. If you sit in one spot you stay at the bottom of the rut. Do the work.

Chapter Nineteen: Monet's Abstract Landscapes

Claude Monet, that great French impressionist, is famous for his light filled landscapes. His gardens, rivers filled with happy sailing scenes and of course his series paintings such as haystacks and Rouen Cathedral.

Monet was fascinated by light and the ephemeral effects it had on the landscape. The air was alive to Monet and he suffered greatly to produce paintings depicting light and air.

For Monet elements like values were sometimes sacrificed for light filled scenes. If you are a values based artist you may suggest that some of his paintings were weak in structure. That would however miss the point. Certainly in a novice a lack of values could lead to weak paintings. But Monet was no ordinary artist. He exemplified impressionist theory and put this to practice in his paintings.

Although Monet is not known for abstract painting it is clear that **abstraction in landscape** was not far off. Consider Monet's series of paintings on the Houses of Parliament in the early 1900's.

Bathed in mist and light the buildings are soft edged silhouettes. Yes the buildings are still clearly recognised as buildings, but the subject was not material structures. The subject was light and the buildings have been reduced to almost flat shapes.

Let's go forward a few years to Monet's later paintings which were almost all done in his garden and around his extensive pond.

The waterlily series moves from depictions that are evident as water lilies to renditions that could be mistaken for modern abstract paintings. Without intending it Monet had started something that would gain momentum with artists like Cezanne. Then to the master of the abstract painting, Pablo Picasso.

There is something here that representational landscape painters can consider too. Recently I wrote about getting out of the creative rut. Trying something new to re-energise.

Why not look at your landscape scene and isolate the shapes. Reduce them to their basic shape and tweak the colours. What is the essence, for example, of long dry grass blowing in the wind?

 What about reflections in a pond or light filtering through leaves. Get up close, squint and note the shapes and also the values of light and dark. Could they be painted? How far into abstraction could you go? Would you feel comfortable doing this?

Contemporary artists like Mitchell Albala paint landscapes with a bias to abstraction. Perhaps expressionist would be more accurate. By selecting different colours and focusing in on the emotional content an ordinary landscape depicting a waterfall could be turned into a billowing spray of light and cloudlike wonder.

You instinctively know that there is an organic process at work which creates an experience for the viewer. More emotional involvement perhaps than merely a spectator.

Give this a go sometime. I am sure that you will learn something new and release some pressure from having to produce a gallery piece in your regular style. You may just end up with a few new tricks to incorporate into your next landscape.

Chapter Nineteen: Is it Time to Reconsider Modern Art

In recent news it was reported that prominent American art critic, Dave Hickey, has "turned his back" on modern art. The article can be read in the UK Guardian. Hickey's scathing comment on the purchasers:

"They're in the hedge fund business, so they drop their windfall profits into art. It's just not serious," he told the *Observer*. "Art editors and critics – people like me – have become a courtier class. All we do is wander around the palace and advise very rich people. It's not worth my time."

Hickey goes on to suggest that a change of outlook in modern art is required:

"Money and celebrity has cast a shadow over the art world which is prohibiting ideas and debate from coming to the fore," he said yesterday, adding that the current system of collectors, galleries, museums and art dealers colluding to maintain the value and status of artists quashed open debate on art.

"I hope this is the start of something that breaks the system. At the moment it feels like the Paris salon of the 19th century, where bureaucrats and conservatives combined to stifle the field of work. It was the Impressionists who forced a new system, led by the artists themselves. It created modern art and a whole new way of looking at things."

Of course I enjoyed the reference to impressionism challenging the status quo of the Paris Salon. So where does art move to from here? If everything has been said already then what is the point of art. I would like to suggest that modern art still has an important part to play in the world.

Whether as social commentary or to tweak the noses of the establishment. I have no problem with art that is committed to its cause by artists with purpose. Whether that cause is to show beauty or satirise a president's backroom antics. **It is about freedom and credibility of art.**

What does not work for me is art that panders to the hedge-fund brigade and the commission-greedy hangers on who cynically promote such works as significant. It is no wonder that prominent art critics feel they cannot win. There is just too much money involved.

Frankly when a critic or art promoter starts punting a living artist's work as "investment art" I get suspicious. If I want an investment I may buy Kruger Rands. If it is art then I will buy what I like to see hanging on my wall. Sure it is nice to know that an artwork will hold its value. But to call it investment art, in most cases, is dishonest marketing.

Do we even need to take note of this state of affairs? After all is it not enough to buy what you like and let everyone get the art they want. The issue is one of credibility. In a world where great and beautiful art is still created by honest artists we need to see that those who influence the art world recognise these artists.

If prominent critics can speak out we will see credibility return to art and that is good for everyone.

Chapter Twenty: Art is Created by Ordinary People Doing Extraordinary Things

How often do we hear people look at a painting and comment about their own lack of ability to draw or paint. It seems like there is a knee-jerk reaction to explain why they do not create art themselves. When I think about it I do wonder if we were not all created to be creative.

Going too far? I'm not so sure, because there is so much art created all the time and in so many forms that the question should be: Why are you not creating art yourself? You can you know and talent should not be wasted.

The comment about not having the ability does not hold water. So let us look further. The reason I suspect has something to do with fear. The one fear is not being good enough from the start and you will look foolish.

There is also the fear of actually being pretty good at first so what comes next? Another painting? What if that is better than the last? What then? This is sometimes called fear of success. A term used by psychologists that I used to find absurd. How could anyone fear success? That is what we all want is it not?

The fear of being a one-hit-wonder. Like <u>Dexys Midnight Runners</u> who wrote Come on Eileen in the eighties. Then having people nag you about when the next album is coming out.

Of course I was much younger and all I wanted was to show that I could be good at something. I had my eye on the moment. Later I would understand that adult's forget about being in the moment.

They look to the future and think what if... and that is scary so they drop the whole thing.

Recently I read an interesting comment that art is created by flawed people. Someone with perfect virtue would not need to create art. I am talking about a saint or superhero. Regular humans are full of faults and vices. No need denying it.

So a regular person full of issues and undesirable qualities creates art. It may be magnificent work, but the thing is the artist is still a regular human being who just happens to plug away at painting or sculpture or song writing. Visit an artist's studio and see the dogs piled up against the wall. Paintings that are not worth the paint used. Sculptures consigned to the recycle bin.

Does the art compensate for something? Is it redemption of sorts? Or maybe it's the human condition and creativity is our God given means to lift ourselves out of the mess. Is there any better way of getting closer to our Maker than to create? I do not believe there is. Not for us regular folks.

There is little doubt that the malaise of daily life lies in people not giving themselves over to creativity. Work in an office? Go home and watch TV - go out and spend money on bright lights and noise. Consume - consume - consume. Consumers. What a word! Sounds like a process of destruction to me. Chomp away until there is nothing left.

What if we try making something? It is hard work, but it fills us up with joy. We do not "follow" our joy - **we make it**. We create and give back and create again.
It is what makes us ordinary people extraordinary.

Chapter Twenty One: Learn from the Past to Create in the Present

Artists are supposed to be unpredictable and spontaneous types. They dress peculiar and do not toe the line. Look back in history. No sooner had the world loosened up a little after the French Revolution did the artists rush to the forefront of rebellion.

Conventions were thrown out like a stale baguette. Enlightened thinking was all the rage and the more outrageous the better. It was not long before artists were all high on absinthe and every manner of misunderstood medication. Or were they?

Sure it is romantic to view artists as strange. There are many artists who covet this label. They do crazy stuff. Put a urinal in a gallery and call it a fountain and lo you are a sensation for your cheeky notions. **I like this myth about artists**.

There is far too much conventional thought going on right now. Thanks to the shenanigans of some greedy financial custodians the world is now run by accountants. Political correctness has turned the lefties into angry loons. Comply or be damned is the new thing.

Not if you are an artist though. Live and let live must still be the rule to ... live by? So let us celebrate the crazy artists and let off some steam.

There is just one thing though. The crazy artists have financial portfolios too (those that have cracked the big time) and the rest of us have internet accounts to pay each month.

We need to have **a system** in place to make this all work. Look at the music scene. Do you think the rolling stones kept on rolling because they were on drugs all the time? Forget it - those guys work a system that has kept them going into old age. Famous artists like Picasso, Monet and too many to mention lived and worked into advanced years. Renoir could barely hold a brush, but kept going until his last moment. Matisse too.

We can learn something about these great artists. They had a system and stuck to it. This system meant they **got to work every day**. They painted following certain rituals in **preparation**. Their minds were free to focus on what mattered. The concept, the light, the brushwork and so on. A chaotic mind leads to a chaotic life and all that is produced is nonsense.

Embrace creativity. Vent your emotions on the canvas or the stage. Write a book that shakes the world. **Take a risk with your art today.** Just keep yourself grounded with a system that works for you. Even lightning needs certain conditions in place before it strikes.

Tips:

1. Avoid being a slave to the news. It is the new opium for the masses;

2. Look inside yourself for what truly moves you;

3. Read and learn from the masters of the past.

4. Avoid procrastination

Chapter Twenty Two: Permission to Create Please?

Calling yourself an artist can be risky. You need to have your wits about you because somebody is going to challenge you and it might come from an unexpected source.

One would think that in this time of democracy we can create with carefree abandon. The tools are there easily within reach. Want to paint? You can buy your paints with a few clicks. Want to write? Start a blog for free!

So what is the problem? Sadly with the release of creativity comes the opposite reaction to block creativity. Does the world need artists? In these times is art not a waste of time and resources? The economy and world peace and so on?

If you can evade these sirens of doubt and create your artwork you then face the gauntlet of opinions designed to drag you down. Is it art? Galleries decide on your future not you! Are you selling? What are your formal qualifications? Is this really going to put food on the table? What will your friends/spouse/parents/colleagues think if you go professional?

If you heed the voices of doubt and give up your art you are telling yourself in no uncertain terms that you cannot go any further without permission. Permission from a host of third parties who are threatened by your decision.

Your courage, although quivering inside, compels you to stand up and declare your art to the world. This will provoke a reaction. Some supportive while others indifferent or downright scornful.

Do you listen and if so to whom?

In truth you can only listen to one voice and that is your own. The voice coming from your soul. The purpose - your path. Not the voice that says you can make money from this or the one that says you will get praise and adulation. These are simply ego trips and will leave you needier than before.

Feeding the ego is a gradual process of disempowerment until the rug is forcibly removed from under your feet and you wonder what the hell happened.

So what? So nothing. Look at yourself and make the choice you need to make. Not what others think or say or do. You and I know deep down that creating is our source of energy. Let us not hand this gift over to others for permission to continue. The next time you hear someone labelling your work or plans in a negative manner know that poison can only kill if you drink it.

A final word is that to accept your gift of energy and power is to acknowledge your duty to work. This is an intensely personal process. Learn and do the work. Live your art every moment and grow day by day.

Chapter Twenty Three: Master of Light

Joaquín Sorolla y Bastida was a Spanish painter. Sorolla excelled in the painting of portraits, landscapes, and monumental works of social and historical themes. Wikipedia

Born: 27 February 1863, Valencia, Spain
Died: 10 August 1923, Madrid, Spain

It may be that the light in Spain reminds me of light in South Africa. It is bold and uncompromising. Light and dark dominates and seldom are there any misty greys to soften the effect.

Since we are entering summer in this part of the world I felt that Sorolla's bold brushwork in this painting evoked the summer mood.

The painting below (*Watching the Fish*, 1907) covers all that I love about Sorolla's painting. Although a tranquil scene we can sense that it was probably a scorching hot day. The cool shadows by the pond bringing some relief. The luminous water, bright reflections, warm pinks and value contrasts all work to illustrate the concept.

In particular the brushwork stands out. Sorolla's brushwork is confident and bold. He was known for assessing and placing his mark then leaving it alone. No blending and fussing which weakens a painting. One can appreciate that the brushwork creates a sensuous texture on the canvas.

This is how oil paint should be used.

Reflected light fills the scene and is closely observed by the artist. Look at the lady's white dress - there is no white paint, but rather a series of greys to convey the shadows and indirect light.

We are also reminded to keep the paint in shadows thinner and transparent while laying it on thick in the brightly lit passages. Overall the harmony of light has been captured and rendered expressively. It is true that we need not worry about harmony if we follow nature's lead and depict colours accurately as they appear in nature. Values and harmony will look real on the canvas too.

We can all learn by studying masters like Sorolla and this should be part of a weekly process when you are in need of a break from painting.

Chapter Twenty Four: No Quick Fix for the Artist

Art is a challenge and the old adage about the more you learn the more you realise that there is still even more to learn, rings true.

A recent art workshop brought this fact home loud and clear. Artists of all abilities share a common cause - the pleasure of creating. We also share the frustrations that this process brings too.

Does the painting you envisage in your mind translate exactly onto canvas? Probably not. Something like the song in your mind seldom sounds right when you sing it out load (that is why my singing is limited to the shower).

Painting is enormously rewarding if you give it the time and space to grow. Talent gets you started and passion fires the soul, but good old dedication and discipline sorts out the pros from the occasional painters. Nothing wrong with whatever direction you choose, however it must be said that **your expectations and effort need to correspond.**

I have learnt over the years that constant practice does bring sweet reward. This could mean doing dozens of drawings, value studies and colour maps before your try out the painting itself.

After years of this process you may be able to refine and distil the preparation somewhat. Occasionally **something so profound strikes** you that you will pick up a brush and create a stunning piece without any preparation at all.

In truth these moments are built on a strong foundation of work.

It is not how much you spend on lessons nor on the extent of your studio equipment. Money cannot buy you effort. That comes from within each artist and we must decide how much we are willing to give. How unsatisfying it would be if painting was a quick-fix thing. A fad for today.

Thankfully painting is hard work and I would not want it any other way.

Chapter Twenty Five: 10 Ways to Unblock Your Creativity

Paint miles of canvas! Just one snag though - it can get a bit stale if you use one approach for weeks or months on end. Without variety in your art process there will not be much progress. Even worse - it might begin to feel like a chore!

The great part about being an artist is the freedom to decide. It is all yours and we sometimes lose sight of this because everything else in life has to be so tight and pc. Cut loose and do something different.

Some ideas

1) **Toning** the canvas the same colours getting you down? Go for multi-colours in loose blocks all over the canvas. What shows through when you are painting may give a new twist;

2) **Drawing** the outlines of your subject in pencil seems ho-hum? Try charcoal and work at arm's length. Get free and loose to show energy and then paint with bold big shapes;

3) **Oil paint again?** Try watercolour. Add some pastels over parts that have dried for a multi-media approach.

4) Change your **palette**: Try painting in monochrome too. This does not have to be black and white, but any colour of your choice. Just vary the values and see what happens. The lessons learnt are priceless.

5) Use different **tools**: Swop the brush for a palette knife for example. Use your fingers to soften edges where required. Use a rag or dry brush technique over dried surfaces to catch the light.

6) **Step outside**. Use a viewfinder and crop any outdoor scene and paint that in twenty minutes. Time yourself. Use a large brush such as size 12 only.

7) **Gallery crawl**: Visit galleries, museums and even artist friends and take a break from your studio for a day or two. Let the experience soak in. Let the juices bubble a bit. Ideas will come. Act on them.

8) **New sights**. Bored with your neighbourhood? You do not need to go on an expensive holiday. Try going for a drive out at a time of day that is not part of your usual routine. For example in summer take an early morning drive or walk (if you are a late riser by habit) and see how the light changes familiar sights.

Another approach is to paint a nocturne - what with there being so much artificial lighting in towns and cities it is possible to paint exciting scenes this way.

9) Do a **self-portrait** with any medium of choice. Simple or detailed - that is up to you. It may reveal more than you think!

10) **Music** - change it - turn it up. Music can light up the creativity in you.

What works for you?

Chapter Twenty Six: Five Truths about Painting

Seeing and drawing what is important is a lesson all artists need to get back to from time to time. The thing about art, and in my case, painting, is that there are many truths that are constant. It is also true that artists, at times, waver and lose focus.

The title refers to five truths yet there are many more, but these five came back to remind me about my personal painting methods. They are as follows:

1) **Make a good start** and the painting is half done before the actual painting gets going. By this I mean that the preparation is still fundamental. Consider the subject and look at the building blocks.

Values: are they interesting? I like strong values and a painting seldom suffers for it. Are the shapes interesting? Do a notan study and outline study to assess the shapes. A few strong shapes should dominate the scene. Only when these basics are accounted for does a painting become possible.

2) **Why am I painting this?** This is a question we must ask ourselves. It is no good just painting something because it has values and shapes. There must be more. Call it the concept or idea behind the painting.

What moves you and how will you convey this with impact? If you feel it then try to make the viewer feel it too. When it comes to landscapes for example I need to be moved by the scene.

It must connect to my soul. I need to feel a deep connection to the beauty or majesty of the scene. Sometimes it is a simple moment of nature that makes a scene magical - the fall of light, the colours and interplay of shadows spark my senses. That is what excites me most about landscapes.

3) **Keep those shapes simple and few**. Nature is perfectly able to pull off a thousand and one shapes and make it look good. Artists however need to keep the shapes few and meaningful. Simplify the scene into a few major shapes - usually seven will do.

Add interest within them and keep them linked with passages of light and dark. Everything must hang together in order to make sense. Far from chaos a painting is a study in order and simplicity.

4) **Keep it Painterly:** Generous paint application is a strength in oil painting. Seldom is a painting spoilt by thick paint and confident brushstrokes. Painterly brushwork is not about details, but about suggestion.

This means that we need not worry about trying to illustrate, but rather to suggest and delight in the medium of generous amounts of paint.

5) **A good painting can be completed quickly**. It is a truth that the best parts of a painting are usually completed within minutes while the boring bits were laboured over for days.

A long time painting does not mean great art. Take your time in preparation, but pull out the stops when the painting begins. Yes a good painting can also seem easy too. These are the paintings that are often the best work. Accept them as the divine moment of creation when all is aligned and beautiful.

Above all - enjoy the process of painting.

Chapter Twenty Seven: Values Add Spice to Art

Did you ever read the children's book Asterix in Britain? I say children's book, but I have read it often enough as an adult too. It is a fantastic work and as satire it is genius. One of the swipes taken at the British is the way they prepare their food. Remember that Asterix is a Belgian work with strong French influences. And Asterix is a Gaul which is to say French.

So our Gaulish heros are familiar with flavour filled food. To their shock they discover that the British like boiled beef! Yuck. And warm beer! Mon Dieu!

Yes bland food is boring. Maybe that is why modern British palates have adopted international food so strongly. Chicken tikka anyone?

It is one of life's truths - to avoid blandness we need to add some spice! Consider this metaphorically and you will see that so much of our life is based on this simple idea. What we eat, read, drive, wear, listen to, in our relationships and in work and play.

We are constantly looking for ways to be more interesting. It seems that this pursuit is never ending unless we can find balance to our lives.

This concept applies to paintings too. We are often drawn to one painting of a subject while ignoring another painting of the same subject. This is common enough, but we can learn much about what attracts us to one of the paintings.

Chances are it relates to the values used by the artist. The elements of contrast between light and dark is so fundamental to a painting's success that I have devoted a sizable portion of my forthcoming workshops to this aspect.

Without a clear understanding of values and how to apply them to a painting we risk producing just another painting lacking in impact. When it comes to spice in art values occupy the red hot section of the spice rack! Use them with care and, but never ignore them.

A good tip is to take up squinting. Before picking up a brush artists need to be able to squint at a subject instinctively to assess the shapes and values. It is worth getting a few strange glances from strangers to learn this fundamental skill.

Then using a 6b pencil rough in the dark shapes in your journal and see what interesting shapes are revealed. For many of you going on holiday this is the perfect time to have a journal and a few pencils on hand. Take a moment every day to try out this technique.

Spice up your paintings with strong values. It will be one of those breakthrough moments that will transform your painting.

Chapter Twenty Eight: Simplicity in All Things

Nature is astonishing. Consider the millions of processes working in our bodies every second without us having to think about it. The life all around us getting on with whatever process is required to sustain itself. Grass grows effortlessly - too effortlessly for my liking in the summer.

The point is that all of nature is following a path of truth and simplicity and is doing so without effort. This to me is the key in so many areas of life. Whenever I try to force something and it seems like so much hard work then I know it is not right. Perhaps it is matter of timing or simply not the course that is correct for me. Nature will have its way and we should try to follow these life rhythms too.

A few weeks ago I tried to paint a scene of hills covered with coastal bush and farm lands. Depending on the time of day the scene is restful and beautiful. Shapes and light make this a great subject.

In my enthusiasm to get started I was painting within half an hour. I had made a quick sketch and considered the composition, but I knew that I was diving in a bit early. Still I went ahead and of course the result was poor. I should have known, but I learnt the same lesson all over again.

Take some time to consider the subject. Look and let yourself get a sense for the atmosphere. I had the luxury of time and had to ease myself into the subject.

After a few days of getting to know the area better and with a few studies done to prepare myself I felt ready to paint the subject again. The results this time were much better. The mood was there and the scene was simplified to what was important for me.

A general landscape needs emotional content to be worth something. So keep the scene simple by leaving out anything that does not add to the mood you are conveying. You can only know what to leave out once you have a feel for the subject itself.

This takes time. But once you have this information the painting almost paints itself. It is effortless and a pleasure to do. These are profound moments that are within the grasp of all of us.

Take a few hours if you can to look at your subject and get to know it at different times of the day. Sure this is not always possible. When time is of the essence then you have to go for it, but if you can revisit a scene then make the effort. It will reward you with a painting that is above your previous level. These are the breakthrough moments and we all need them.

It is also about learning your craft as an artist.
It is about intentional thinking and execution of a concept.

Chapter Twenty Nine: Five Truths Part 2

Recently I wrote about five truths in painting. After a month dedicated to painting, thinking and writing about art I have five more items to add to this list.

1. **Retail Therapy is a lie!** My family was fortunate to be away from the malls this holiday season. I do not want to sound like a Grinch, but less time around shops is good for the soul not to mention the pocket.

   How does this relate to art? Time and peace for creative work! More creative work makes me a happy guy and my family is happier too. Honestly shopping is a distraction, which we all know is just procrastination. Plus the time saved beggars belief. A quick shopping expedition takes two hours!

2. **If you have to force it then it was probably wrong to begin with.** Great art is effortless. Have I gone mad! No - let me put it this way. It may seem like a ton of work looking in from the outside, but to the artist in the sublime moment of creation it is effortless.

   All creation is effortless. Nature does not struggle - creation is happening all the time without any difficulty. Our simple attempts at art pale in comparison. Take a look at a painting you have done that you are particularly happy with. There is probably a portion of the painting that you are very pleased with. It happened without any trouble.

You may wonder if you could ever duplicate that moment of mastery. Now there will be other parts of the painting that took some labour. It is likely that those parts look it too - laboured I mean.

3. **If you want good things to happen then you must give good things too.** Art requires sincerity. Paint for the love of art. Not envy or for competition. True art or any form of creation cannot be achieved any other way.

4. **Time is irrelevant:** To the creative process time is unimportant. Some artists put a lot of store in saying something like: "I have been painting for twenty years!" So what? What counts is what you do with your moment of creation.

   Create art with intention and focus and keep at it. Every day should have some action related to your art. The mastery of art cannot be achieved any other way and trust me it will happen, but you will still want more since the creative spirit never dies.

5. **Take Responsibility:** Progress in our art is up to us alone. Teachers can only open a window for us to look into a part of their world. It is our duty to learn from as many sources as possible.

   Accept and reject what you want, but never blame others for your difficulty in technique or process. I sometimes hear part-time artists name dropping about art lessons with so-and-so or suggesting that a teacher did not show them how to do something or other.

Certainly there is self-sufficiency in all artists who are in it for the long haul. My experience suggests to me that only those who keep their focus on self-development and take full responsibility for this make it in the end.

The opportunities for learning are infinite. All that matters is that we take these opportunities and remember to be grateful for them.

Chapter Thirty: Landscapes Help You to Paint Better Portraits

A participant of one of my online workshops noted that I painted many landscapes. She wanted to know if I could help her paint portraits too. I answered that I could and briefly spoke about the universal approach to painting irrespective of the subject. It was a good question and needs a fuller response.

My workshop covers many aspects of painting, but there is perhaps one central theme. **Learning how to see like an artist.** This has to be learnt through conscious practice over time. Innate talent is within us all. To unleash this talent effectively requires intention and practice.

Nobody can teach originality or style. Those qualities are the happy burden for each artist to carry. But learning to see like an artist can be taught to the willing student.

How does this relate to portrait painting? Simply this - a portrait or figure study is an arrangement of shapes in various hues and values. There is also the gesture of the person although this covers more than technique. Most students will be focused on technique at first and this is fine to begin with.

Not convinced? Painting landscapes is challenging. There is good reason why so many great artists have spent so much time painting the great variety of subjects that nature provides.

Light, seasons, colours and moods fill our natural world with variety on a daily basis if not hourly. No wonder that we love landscapes so much. Look closer and it is clear that an artist must be able to see accurately, evaluate and make decisions about shapes, hues and values not to mention placement of brushstrokes.

If painting plein air then these decisions must be made quickly. These skills apply to portrait painting too.

Yes there is some license given to the landscape artist to leave out elements that distract and if a tree is "moved" for better composition then this may be forgiven too.

However painting a likeness in a portrait requires accurate recording of shapes in their proper place. This is when the hours of training the eye to see accurately will help the artist.

Manet's portrait of Berthe Morisot is an example of painterliness that conveys a likeness and intrigues us with shapes of colour and brushwork when viewed closer.

The bold contrasts between light and dark shapes is an important approach for every landscape artist too. It bears mentioning that Manet was also an accomplished landscape artist.

Another benefit to the landscape artist is the ability to work with a larger brush to carve out planes and surfaces. A comparison to sculpture with a brush instead of a chisel is helpful to illustrate this approach.

This **avoids the overly rendered photo-realist approach** that in so many cases results in a dull surface (note the protests over the Dutchess of Cambridge's portrait). Would Manet's approach have been better to capture something more intangible?

Colour notes placed carefully yet expressively in shaping a portrait is, to my view, more desirable and interesting than overly-rendered realism. But that is a matter of choice.

It must also be said that painting from life instead of a photograph will give better results. Many landscape artists have developed this skill outdoors. There can be no messing about with fiddly details outdoors. This helps in portrait painting too. Give it a try.

Painting is an adventure and any limits are self-imposed. Paint what makes you joyful and try many different subjects to really grow as an artist.

Chapter Thirty One: The Artist's Solution

Would you take on a trek in the wild with a guide who only knew how to do one thing really well? Your guide can make a fire from almost anything. But sadly he cannot read a map, the stars and has a rather poor sense of direction. You would be warm but you would stay lost too.

There was a time when being a specialist was the ideal. We were told that specialised training and university degrees were the ticket to lifelong prosperity. At least we would be comfortable and have a good pension plan. If you had a problem then a specialist would be called in to solve it. This was good. Everyone knew the rules.

But things have changed. Suddenly it seems that the specialist looks out of place. The man in the shiny suit and tie looking dazed at the interest rates on the mortgage bond account. I have read that one must be able to select something, anything, and be really good at it. An expert.

But is that enough? I suspect not. **These days you need to be more than an expert in one thing.** You need to be an expert is something and very good in many others and still competent in even more areas.

This will mean being able to do your primary claim to fame, market yourself, master technology, fix the leak in the roof, mend the door and cook a healthy meal. If you cannot do these things you may need an artist to help you.

No really. What is an artist? He or she need not be a painter or singer (although they could be). A true artist is an enthusiastic **problem solver**.

Take painting for example. Every painting is a series of problems and corrections until finally the artist is satisfied with the solution. Once the painting is completed the solution is not forgotten.

Then the painting must get to market and be sold so that the artist can buy paints and pay the electricity bill. Problem to be solved - how to market and sell in a hostile economy. How to thrive in times when uncertainty prevails? How to update your website gallery? These are complex problems and require multiple skills to arrive at a solution.

How does this apply to the world today? Simply this - every person today needs to up their skills. The general practitioner in life will prevail while the specialist will become vulnerable.

What happens when your employer demands that you relocate to another city? Can you refuse and keep your job? If not you are vulnerable unless you can find a solution within your skills and other abilities.

There is an artist within everyone. This is a fact that can be seen in people a century or two ago. Before **production lines and timer clocks made us helpless**. We have to face a new time where self-sufficiency is required to survive. We need to become artists once again.

Chapter Thirty Two: Art, Freedom and Tyranny

Liberty, n. One of Imagination's most precious possessions.(Ambrose Bierce)

When the government or other established power bases start to challenge any art form, including freedom of speech and information, I see weakness and desperation in that government. When the guardians of freedom of speech voluntarily or unwittingly put themselves into the hands of powerful interests then we are in trouble. Big trouble!

When art is accepted at best and tolerated at worst it may suggest a healthy society. People get on with their lives and can think for themselves (without the powers that be trying to control these thoughts).

Artists are happy to accept or ignore different opinions on what they produce. That is the way it should be and everybody gets on with life. But when art is condemned by a ruling power then there is poverty of leadership.

Recently I was researching impressionist art. One of the books spent time on the revolution in art and ideas that gave birth to impressionism.

One major catalyst of course was the art academy trying to control what art when on exhibition at the annual Salon. This official recognition was critical to making a living as an artist.

If you were rejected you quite literally could starve unless you gave up art and took up another trade. Modern self-promotion and galleries did not exist.

Understandably when the world started entering modern times artists started to resist these shackles. **Change was inevitable.**

Fast forward to 1930's Germany. The Nazi government tries to stamp out art forms it terms "degenerate". At first the Nazis try to do this by humiliating the artists. The Nazis seize the paintings and mount a travelling exhibition in Germany and Austria. Tens of thousands flock to see the art that is *verboten*. Why is the art so popular? Sure many are simply curious, but is there something to art as a catalyst for ideas and a symbol of freedom when this human right is under threat. Why were the Nazis so fearful of artistic expression that did not meet their approved propaganda? **Is art powerful after all?**

As time has moved forward with greater technological change it has become easy to laugh off art as a weekend activity. A hobby. Art students are tolerated and even pitied for being naive. We need professionals and engineers. So why is it time for artists to recognise their power? What is missing in this modern society?

For one thing people feel that their back is against the wall. Regulation of everything, massive price increases, no job security and tough competition means everyone must look out for themselves. Technology can mean freedom or enslavement. It is up to the individual to choose and choice can be scary.

When we see government attacking an artist's work, attacking free speech in television adverts, threatening journalists with action if they seek the truth then perhaps we are seeing a new appreciation for the power of ideas.

Ideas expressed in art has power when we recognise that all is not well in our daily lives. Art can jolt society out of its torpor. Art is creativity in action and it does provoke at an emotional level. Tyrants know that ideas are dangerous.

What is this brief rant about? Simply this - **do not trust authority when it attacks art.** When it tries to control arts and media. When it tries to ridicule artists. Art cannot be imprisoned. Art is within us. **Art is freedom and art is critical to the world today.** The next time leaders with feet of clay cry out indignantly at an artist, do not fall for it. The emperor does indeed have no clothes.

Chapter Thirty Three: Top Three Blocks to Creativity

> The Process of becoming unstuck requires tremendous courage, because we are completely changing our way of perceiving reality. (Pema Chodron)

Creative blocks happen to all artists. How can anyone possibly be blocked from doing something that they love? The creative block comes in many shapes and forms and seems to adapt itself to each person. The quote above is spot on. Our perception of reality is what this is all about. If you perceive an obstacle to getting the work done then the obstacle is real to you.

What are the most common blocks to artists? The top three blocks appear to be:

1. **I do not have the time!** There can be little argument that this is a very common reason. It is probably the excuse that everyone has used at some time. We can all relate to being under time pressures. Demands on our precious time can destroy our energy for creativity. But if we are honest with ourselves do the time pressures arise every day or every hour? What about tomorrow when the deadline is over?

   Chances are another time pressure takes its place. I read a great comparison put forward by marketing guru Marcus Sheridan the other day.

He said that we always find time to do the books because the consequences are dire if we do not. However when our creative time is at stake we do not take it seriously enough. Sadly this becomes a habit after a while and we cannot see our way out of the perceived reality.

This is where the bravery comes in. We need to test these perceptions and see if they are real. Sheridan asks the question - do you have time to watch a TV show? Yes? Then you have time for doing something creative too.

2. **It is a waste of time!** Ouch! When we see that there is time we tend to smack ourselves down anyway. This is especially when money gets in the way. When sales are slow or non-existent for months at a time it is difficult to justify painting.

   Costs of materials suddenly seem like millstones weighing us down. Perhaps a real job will keep the coffers ticking along. Other self-defeating mantras come into play too. Perhaps a negative family member throws in a comment that sounds like "I told you so!" Books have been written about this topic as it covers more than creative blocks, but also businesses of all types go through this when money dries up.

   All that we can do is look at this issue as objectively as possible and push on through. Rains always arrive after the drought.

3. **Negative Feedback has killed your creativity:** Especially when it comes from someone whom we thought would be supportive. Wherever it comes from negative feedback hurts. What we do with it is up to us though.

It helps to look at any feedback to see if it is actually constructive criticism. If constructive then use it as far as is reasonable. Always keep an eye on your goals and objectives when creating.

Sometimes the critic misses the point. It is the artist who must remain the final arbiter. Trouble follows if we create to please others. Where a critic is malicious then reject the feedback for what it is. The choice then is clear and we need to move on.

We will always have challenges to face when art is our calling. It has always been that way. But what is the alternative? Not creating? I don't think so.

Chapter Thirty Four: Get it Down Quickly!

"*He who hesitates is lost*" is a well-known proverb attributed to the 18th century essayist Joseph Addison. The meaning is clear - take too long to deliberate and you will miss an opportunity. Others will argue that a moment to reflect will save you from acting too rashly. No wonder life can get complicated!

Thankfully painting has opened so many avenues of knowledge for me. Dealing with risk is one of them. Compared to other things the risks in painting seems worth taking. So often artists get caught out by the fear of messing up a painting that the result is inevitable. The painting is lost and worse yet - the new artist's confidence has taken a beating too.

It is strange that we can be so harsh on ourselves. I have yet to meet the Art Police and nobody seems to actually care that much if I throw out a painting. It is me, my paints and a canvas. Oh yes - that voice in the mind that fuels my doubts.

Did you know that we are hardwired to look for problems and fears even if these do not exist in reality? This has something to do about survival. It makes sense when we look at our early ancestors living short and brutal lives in the wild. Yet despite our advances in all areas of existence the unfounded fears persist. A massive boon for newspapers and medication companies!

Let us look at art again. Once we can see where our fears come from (hardwired response) and understand that they are unfounded we can give free reign to our creative drive.

What are the risks? Criticism - so what! Who are we trying to please through our art? There is only one direct beneficiary from our artistic efforts and that is ourselves going through the process of creating.

Purchasers or admirers of our work (bless them) have their own personal benefits and the artist cannot be a part of this. An artist simply channels a process. Then it is over and the energy passes on when the art is shared.

One useful way to increase your painting confidence is to paint quick studies. No more than half an hour on a small panel (20cm x 25cm) preferably outdoors. The idea is to get something down quickly - an impression of what is actually there.

This focus on the moment shuts out the incessant doubts that you mind throws at you. By using a large brush - size 8 - 10, you prevent yourself from getting caught up in little details too. Squint to see the large shapes of light and dark and try to get the colours and values correct then put them on the canvas.

Do not worry too much about getting the colours or values spot-on. If they are not correct you will take this knowledge and learn from it before moving onto the next quick study. I may mention here that a hundred or so quick studies should get you on the right track.

Do the doubts ever go away? Of course not - I did mention that they are hardwired in our mind so we need to be aware. **Awareness is the key to freeing ourselves.** Painting with freedom and spontaneity is a constant challenge that opens our minds to life's bigger picture. Most hurdles are figments of our imagination so ignore the doubts.

Instead, let us create.

Chapter Thirty Five: When to Push Your Painting Style

There is a unique signature style in every artist. When starting out this style is in its infancy, but it will mature and change with time. Much like us as we grow up over time our appearance changes too. Our art will develop as we take on new ideas, methods and throw off others. This is healthy. We have to keep on learning and trying new things to give ourselves a chance of fulfilling our potential.

I have said before that nobody can teach you a style of painting, but you can accept and reject as you please. If you are true to yourself your own signature will come to you. The potential that we all have to adapt and grow in our art is huge. In fact I am beginning to think that it is only by our choice that we encounter limits. Sometimes these choices are conscious and other times unconscious.

Perhaps some fear, discomfort or event steps in and we experience a detour. We can choose to get back on track or not. When I see or read about extraordinary achievements by those who have huge hurdles to overcome, whether physical or in their circumstances, then I am convinced that I am capable of so much more.

A few years ago I read a fascinating book called E=mc2 by David Bodanis. It is an explanation of Einstein's legacy and the development of his theory of relativity written for average-joe (me) to understand.

Among the mind bending facts about the abundance of energy in the universe was an example of the potential energy in any mundane item, like a sheet of paper. If this energy could be released it would flatten a city.

Can there be any doubt that each tiny atom making up our very existence is part of the universe's infinite power?

Within us is the power and energy of the sun! Seems the least I could do is watch a little less TV and paint something nice.

On the subject of potential it is every artist's privilege to interpret a subject according to his or her concept. If an artist likes representational art does this mean that the subject must not be changed at all?

In my view every subject should be pushed a bit or as much as is necessary to convey the emotional response. Although I spend much time teaching how to mix colours and get values correct this is not to turn anyone into a boring painter.

The idea is that by knowing colour and value you will be able to ramp these up or modify them to give a painting energy and impact. You need to know the differences to make the best decision.

There is so much potential energy and life to be conveyed in a painting. If a colour does not convey your feeling then give it more beans! There is nothing wrong with this if the relationships between colours, shapes and values are all in synch.

Remain true to your concept and feeling and do not hold back.

Chapter Thirty Six: Where Do Painting Ideas Come From?

A popular question from collectors is where do I get the ideas for paintings? This may relate to the subject or the colours used or any other aspect of a painting. I often laugh off these questions simply because there is not a ready answer.

The immediate answer sounds too trite. The truth is that stimulating ideas are part of each artist's process and it is helpful to know what fuels your idea engine.

I am firstly attracted to subjects that have elements of strong lights and darks. Secondly a good design that will draw in the eye and keep the viewer interested. The third leg is that emotional connection that is much more difficult to define. Without it however the painting has little chance of survival. This makes commissions so tricky. There must be a spark for me to give it any justice.

Having accepted that I cannot paint a scene that does not move me there are others ways to get the ideas flowing.

I need a positive frame of mind for starters. Some artists want to show the grim side of life, but that does not work for me. There is no radio news, TV or newspapers in my studio. They kill my creativity.

I need positive energy and usually nature provides that for me. I guess that explains my love of landscapes. All I need is to take a drive out of town. It is a case of wanting to stop every kilometre to capture a scene.

It has become a joke for my family. I am considering mounting a camera on my dashboard!

Waiting for inspiration? This does not work for me either. Inspiration shows up when I get working. Preparing painting boards, stretching a canvas or just cleaning up the studio can get the ideas ticking over. If I get a good idea I will go out and look for the scene.

For example I have just been working on a seascape. The idea was simple enough, but went a lot deeper into my personal nature. It was the idea of staring out at the sea, which I can easily do for an hour, and letting the shapes, shadows and light form images in the mind. Free thought similar to what you get from staring at clouds. In any case I then headed off to the beach on a cloudy day and watched the sea. That was all I needed with a few notes and I could work on a larger studio painting.

Other times I will set up an easel outdoors in an area that appeals to me. Then using a viewfinder I will look for a composition that has all the strong visual elements that I like. Whatever approach I follow is part of a working process. It is not a case of watching TV, for example, and an idea pops into my head. *Creative processes lead to more creativity.*

I am never worried about running out of ideas. I do not believe in creative block and so on. It comes down to a choice and then getting to work. If I do not do the work then there will be little in the ideas department.

Chapter Thirty Seven: To Find Meaning and Make a Living with Art

A comment sent to me by a fellow artist struck me as a universal statement for any artist trying to make a go of an art career.

"I am a returning artist struggling to make a sale, I am not sure if it is my paintings, price, subject or my selling techniques. Any help greatly appreciated."

I can relate to this heart felt plea. When artists get down on themselves it is often verbalised along the lines of "I am not making sales, because my art is not good enough" or "If I can sell ___x___ paintings this weekend I am OK". When the target is not met then it is so easy to blame yourself.

The truth must be faced before we can get into career strategy. In truth an artist needs recognition at a fundamental level. This gets confused with sales as a yardstick, but this is a mistake. Sales alone will not fill the need for recognition.

A better way of saying this is that the artist needs to know that his art is actually good. The trap with sales as a yardstick is that the artist becomes attached to numbers and when they do not add up to a certain sum the artist takes this as a rejection. **If it is numbers you are after then there will never be enough.**

I know a few artists (I use the word loosely) who knowingly churn out paint-by-numbers style works for the quick sale. They freely admit to this and laugh it off. The problem is that they are not selling art. There is no true communication. It is a lie and they are caught up in a numbers game that is now their life. If they do not get back to the truth of art they will fade away disillusioned.

Art is firstly a form of communication. **The meaning of communicating through art is achieved when the artist's efforts are recognised.**

Painting sales alone will never fill the artist's soul. So when we are not attached to sales as a yardstick we can accept the ups and downs of business a lot better. It is not the artist's talent that is at fault. If no sales take place then artists must make business decisions to rectify the situation. Not throw their hands up in despair and curse their imagined lack of talent.

Let me add that improving skills and quality of art is a business decision too. These are learned qualities through effort not a marker for abundance or lack of talent. Artists have the talent, but must add the sweat to hone the skill.

Attachment to an outcome leads to frustration. Reality and our imagined outcome seldom meet halfway. Instead if we focus our efforts on doing the work as best as we can with a lightness of spirit we will not fall into the trap. Artists will benefit from calmer minds and they will be kinder to themselves. Their work will improve consistently.

This idea of non-attachment is not easy especially over the long haul. Our commercial world has seen to that. Being aware helps to foresee trouble so that we can head it off. If the artist stumbles over a bad habit like feeling sorry for himself then it will also be easier to pull himself out of it and get back to work.

There is no communication if there is no art. Once the art is produced it must be shared and once shared a connection is made, which in turn brings meaning to the artist's efforts.

So the goal is to improve the artist's communication through art to a wider audience on a regular basis. This must be the intention. It is not accidental. Collectors seek communication with an artist too so step one is to get the conversation going.

Chapter Thirty Eight: The Joy of the Unexpected Moment

Saturday morning very often means one thing in suburbia - shopping day. Of course there are a few people who will argue that they do more than shop, but the throngs of cars heading to the malls suggests shopping is big.

This activity is a necessary evil yet I am not alone in trying to minimise the impact shopping has on my precious free time. I am blessed in having a wife who shares these sentiments. We will be the ones waiting outside the shop's doors as they are opened by bleary eyed shop assistants. The aim being for us to get in and out as fast as possible before the crowds arrive.

This past Saturday was an exception. Neither my wife nor I could face this weekly expedition. The weather was cool and the wind was absent for a change. Only one thing for it - grab the paint kit and head off to the beach for an hour or three of painting.

This was not entirely selfish since my children came with too and they could get some fresh air while I did my thing with the paints.

My choice was well rewarded. Several other people had come down to the beach too and there was a good deal of surfers taking advantage of the magnificent waves. If this sounds idyllic then let me confirm it - **it really was fantastic**. A moment where time flies by as you become lost in doing something you love.

Soon into my second painting I noticed a gentleman emerging from the surf who had been boogie boarding. Turns out he was on retirement and had started painting. He joined me to chat about art and we shared a few stories about our favourite topic.

A few things learnt on that morning:

- It really is not difficult to try something new like painting outdoors. Make it easier by choosing a fair weather day.
- The sense of communing with nature is worth the effort
- You never know who you might meet and where that shared experience may take you.

Lessons from nature:

- The sea is seldom made up of perfectly curling viridian waves with see through bits. It is more often grey or dark blue/green. You will learn to see what is actually there. Not some formulaic seascape.
- Beach sand has many colour variations - at least five or six colours with value changes. It is often a dirtier version with bits and pieces of jetsam, beach grass and footprints that give more interest than some postcard fantasy. Decide what to leave in and what stays out, but see it and make a decision. This is what builds painting confidence.

Not every plein air foray is a success, but the same can be said of the studio too. Make it part of your overall painting experience to get a balanced view of landscape painting.

Or you could try shopping at the mall instead. Nah!

Chapter Thirty Nine: Artists Must Remain Independent

Recently I received an e-mail from a third year university art student. This student told me his subject majors and then proceeded to ask me for employment after he graduates this year.

I am always happy to hear from other artists sharing their experiences and so forth, but this was a first for me. Clearly I am in no position to hire other artists. Perhaps Damien Hirst needs artists to manufacture his next installation, but my studio has to make do with me flying solo.

Sure I do appreciate that income is critical for so many. I do assume that the purpose of a degree is to prepare one for some sort of independence to earn an income. Naive I know. A day job does give a measure of security. It was not always this way. There was a time when you were your own boss first - especially artists.

Everything changed when the world became geared to churning out employees. That was the model from the industrial revolution and it worked wonders for two hundred years. Factories can churn out widgets by the thousand using machines and basic skilled labour to pack the widgets or sort them on the conveyor belt.

Managers would make sure targets were met. Accountants would tally up debits and credits and lawyers would keep the paperwork in order. But all of this order was shaken up by globalisation and the internet.

Fanatical new economies rose up and threatened the happy dream. Now pensions and job security are disappearing. The political elite saw to it that we remained fearful and dependent.

But we do not have to accept this world view.

We need to be our own expert and general practitioner again. Every tool necessary for self-fulfilment is available to us. Artists should know this, but have we been dreaming too? Have we been fed the idea that all you needed for success is an art degree, some paintings and a gallery will snap up your work and you will be set for life?

Was this student under the impression that a job was necessary to take off with his career? It is possible perhaps to land a plush mentorship with a big name artist or maybe an assistant in a metropolitan gallery, but highly unlikely.

What did this suggest about the art degree and our education system? Was this student not taught the fundamentals of marketing and business so that he could stand up for himself in the big world out there? What about the talent within that young artist - genius even - that needed to be unleashed from the confines of academe to take the world by storm? If the youthful artists are not doing this then who will?

The old system of jobs and security is long gone. There is no security in the gallery system either. The established galleries are hanging on, the rest have closed down and self-marketing has taken care of the vast bulk of artists out there.

Today a gallery may get twenty people in a day browsing through. But online an artist actively marketing his work may get three thousand visitors. Yes there are challenges using this approach, but the numbers do not lie. The system has changed forever. On the bright side **we now have all this opportunity.**

It is time that all artists forget about security in a system long dead and embrace the freedom that being an artist suggests. Stand up for yourself and make your way by doing good work and setting your own course.

Chapter Forty: When to Quit a Painting?

There is no point in continuing with a flawed painting. Life is too short. Learn your lessons and move on, wiser and stronger. (anon)

Art is never finished, only abandoned. (Leonardo da Vinci)

A life spent chasing other people's approval is a life spent on a pointless roller coaster of emotional highs and lows, without ever knowing yourself. (Rinatta Paries)

The old joke is that there are two people necessary to complete a painting. The artist to paint it and someone to drag the artist away when the painting is done. Richard Schmid, the famous American artist jokes in his book, *Alla Prima*, about receiving gentle threats from his loved ones should he not stop on a particular painting for risk of ruining it.

There are other reasons to quit too. Not least of which is that the painting will be ruined. Perhaps it never had a chance and you should cut your losses? Recognising the critical moment is the elusive key.

"Do not consider your painting finished unless it is exactly what you want to see. If you feel that you are not skilled enough to do that, take the time and trouble to learn what it is you need to know to do it" says Schmid.

These are tough words from the master artist. A reminder to us all that the path to accomplished painting is a long one.

When I am facing a slump in my painting it can be difficult to pull myself out of it if I dwell on the learning that still lies ahead. So I find it best to take a break and usually by the next day a solution to the problem shows itself. There is always a solution if you keep your mind open to this idea.

Even though there is a solution this does not necessarily mean I can plough on with a flawed painting. The solution may require scraping the whole thing down and starting over.

If that is what it takes then I do not hesitate. If the previous attempts have dried and scraping is not an option then out the painting goes. Learn from it and move on. These dogs are not pets - they must be released!

The typical painting killers are:

No concept - this means there was no idea of what the artist wanted to achieve. What do you want to say about your subject? If your concept is clear you will have an idea of what the focus area of the painting is. Concentrate on the focus area and leave the rest of the painting loose. Nothing can be achieved by rendering the painting in detail from edge to edge of the canvas.

Not enough preparation - for the beginner this can include fundamentals like completing a notan sketch, outline drawings and value studies. All these missed steps lead to poor composition, weak colour and aimless pushing of paint around the canvas.

Too uptight - once the groundwork is done then crack on and paint quickly and with purpose. Wet-into-wet still works best. When we let a painting dry over a week or so it is difficult to get back into it. It is like starting all over again and much changes in the interval. Suddenly the spark of life has left the painting.

Overwork - you have made a good start but now you have gone too far. The details are too rendered and the life has given way to overworked stodge. This is common through all painting levels so do not beat yourself up about it.

Be aware of the moment when you look at your work and think Wow! That is looking great! **It is at that moment** when you must consider whether there is anything more to say. Can adding something now actually add meaning to the painting? If not then stop. If in doubt - sleep on it. Next morning the solution may simply be to sign the painting.

Good luck!

Beginnings and Thank You

I am not sure where my desire to create comes from. Besides from the universal power that creates us all, of course. I am told the arty side of the family tree is rooted in my paternal grandmother's side. I do recall from a very young age watching my father draw quick cartoons on the back of cigarette boxes. Back in the early seventies. It was fascinating to see this. The first inkling at the magic of art.

Thank you gran and whoever came before.

I also am grateful to all those people who have encouraged me along the way. Some family has been worried and other members have been supportive. Nothing unusual about that.

Friends during school days and beyond who appreciated my artistic side for creating pictures, designs and others amusements for them. It is always fun doing this.

And my wife for supporting my art even though it meant risk to her as well. Thank you.

And to you who have read to this point. I am honoured to have your support. Thank you.

Malcolm Dewey

www.malcolmdeweyfineart.com

About

Malcolm Dewey is a South African artist working in various mediums including oils, watercolor and pastel. Malcolm paints mostly landscapes in an impressionist style.

He is the author of a number of instruction books and art marketing books. Malcolm enjoys teaching art and has produced several online courses for beginners and intermediate artists. He also holds live workshops.

More information can be found at Malcolm's website www.malcolmdeweyfineart.com

Printed in Poland
by Amazon Fulfillment
Poland Sp. z o.o., Wrocław

60545604R00066